HOW TO BE A SUCCESSFUL BLACK MAN

Written by **Daniel Laroche**
Illustrated by **James Christy Bazile**

How to be a Successful Black Man

Copyright 2021 @Daniel Laroche, MD

Published by Daniel Laroche MD
49 West 127th Street
New York, NY,10027
dlarochemd@gmail.com

Library of Congress Control Number: 2021908953

ISBN# 978-0-578-84177-9

Published in the United States

ACKNOWLEDGEMENT

I wish to thank my late father Daniel Laroche MD Sr from Port au Prince, Haiti and my mother Lise Beaulieu Laroche from Montreal, Canada for their love and guidance throughout my life to give me better opportunities for success. I wish to acknowledge the late Dr. Ivan Van Sertima, the late Dr. John Henrik Clarke, and the late Dr. Yosef Ben Jochannan. Their many scholarly literary works on the African origin and history of spirituality, science, culture have been tremendously inspirational in my success and knowledge of self. If you have not already read their work, I highly encourage you to do so. I would also like to acknowledge the scholarly teachings of Jabari and Anika Osaze with the Shrine of MAAT for their work in rebuilding the Kemetic legacy. Finally, I want to thank my wife Marjorie and my children Ariel and Gabrielle for their love and support. May this book be the beginning of your journey to learn more about the glorious history of the Nile Valley, Kemet and Kush and incorporate the teaching of our ancestors towards your personal and societal success.

My name is King Menes.
I live in 3000 BCE before the
common era.
I am the first king of Kemet and
Kush (now known as Egypt) in
Africa that unified the North and
South into one kingdom. It is
important to know your history
and your worth.

DID YOU KNOW THAT CIVILIZATION STARTED IN AFRICA?

We all are descendents from a Black woman known as Lucy from the land now know as Ethiopia, formerly known as Kemet and Kush.

- Civilization started in Africa 200,000 years ago.
- 150,000 years ago inhabitants began leaving Africa to populate the rest of the world
- As the glaciers melted the continent of Africa connected to Mesopotamia allowing migration
- Africa provided the foundation for Science, Technology, Religion and Life.
- All people have some percentage of their DNA that comes from Africa.

THE NUBIAN PHARAOHS

BLACK KINGS ON THE NILE

RELIGION IS AN IMPORTANT PART OF OUR SOCIETY AND YOU MUST KNOW IT ORIGINATED FROM THE BELIEF SYSTEMS AND SPIRITUALITY IN AFRICA

- Amun (we now say Amen) was the original powerful God in Africa.
- The first Trinity was Ausar, Auset and Heru.
- This is evolved to Judaism and Christianity.

Auset   Ausar   Heru
Isis   Osaris   Horus
Mary   Holy Ghost   Jesus

• Akhenaten was the founder of monotheism, the belief in one god, the sun god

• The Ankh was the original cross in Africa.

Did you know MAAT had 42 admonitions, or commandments, and that MAAT originated in Africa?

• These teachings existed for 2000 years before the Ten Commandments of Moses.

• MAAT was a female deity.

• MAAT formed the foundation of Judaism, Christianity, Islam and many other religions around the world that have emerged since.

"It is Important to Know Your Roots"

•First and foremost, you must know that we live in a world that teaches people the false doctrine of white supremacy

•Schools around the world teach with images of a white God, a white Jesus

•Schools, media and society falsely teach and promote that Whites are smarter than Blacks, and that Blacks were only slaves and not the founders of civilization in Africa

•White supremacy was set up to profit from people of color

Why is it Important to Know the Truth About Your Roots?

•Once you are aware of this artificial white supremacy you will not have low self esteem
•You will be more confident
•You will feel more secure and be better able to navigate your way to success

MANY HISTORICAL LEADERS MARCHED AGAINST BLACKS

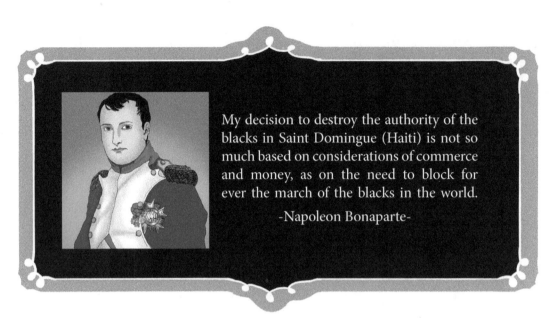

My decision to destroy the authority of the blacks in Saint Domingue (Haiti) is not so much based on considerations of commerce and money, as on the need to block for ever the march of the blacks in the world.

-Napoleon Bonaparte-

Is it important to have a strong sense of self?

• With the false teaching and promotion of white supremacy, some feel that by trying to be white they will be more accepted and less discriminated against.

Modern Religion Has Been Corrupted

• Many White people continue to practice racial discrimination against Blacks today and deny the African foundation of civilization.

Be careful of slavery in the Torah

• The Hebrew bible contains two sets of rules governing slaves: one set for Hebrew slaves (Lev. 25:39-43) and a second set for Canaanite slaves (Lev. 25:45-46). The main source of non-Hebrew slaves were prisoners of war.

• Hebrew slaves, in contrast to non-Hebrew slaves, became slaves either because of extreme poverty (in which case they could sell themselves to an Israelite owner) or because of inability to pay a debt. There is no slavery in the admonitions of MAAT.

Beware of plagiarizing and corruption of the African Spiritual System

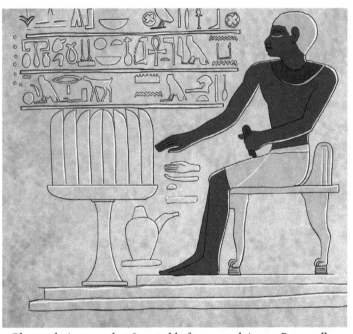

Phararoh Amenemhat I seated before sacred Amen-Ra candles.

Kwanzaa candles are a modern restoration of the African's Amen-Ra candals.

The Hebrew Africans had Amen-Ra candals became known as Men-o-Ra candals.

•Many Christians have practiced land theft from native Indigenous people, practiced slavery and colonialism against Blacks. They have also created Jesus as a white image of the Son of God.

Did you know there is Slavery mentioned in the Bible?

• Ephesians 6:5: "...Slaves, obey your earthly masters with respect and fear and sincerity of heart just as you would show Christ. And do this not to please them while they are watching, but as servants of Christ, doing the will of God from your heart..."

Did you know that according to the Koran, Islam allowed slavery?

• The Prophet Muhammad had slaves, and they included: Safivya bin Huyayy, whom he freed and married; Maria al-Qibtivva, given to Muhammad by a Sassanid official, whom he freed and who may have become his wife; Sirin, Maria's sister, whom he freed and married to the poet Hassan bin Thabit and Zayd ibn Harithah, whom Muhammad freed and adopted as a son.

Did you know that many Muslims have stolen land from Africans and practice modern day slavery in Libya against Blacks?

IS IT IMPORTANT TO LEARN ABOUT THE LAWS OF MAAT?

In Chapter 125 of *The Papyrus of Ani*, we find the petitioner led by Anubis into duat and pronouncing his/her 42 affirmative declarations, listed below from Budge's public domain translation of the 42 Divine Principles of MAAT:

- I have not committed sin
- I have not committed robbery with violence.
- I have not stolen.
- I have not slain men or women.
- I have not stolen food.
- I have not swindled offerings.
- I have not stolen from God/Goddess.
- I have not told lies.
- I have not carried away food.
- I have not cursed

Ankh

Symbol
of
Life

THESE TEACHINGS PROVIDE A GREAT SPIRITUAL FOUNDATION:

- I have not closed my ears to truth.
- I have not committed adultery.
- I have not made anyone cry.
- I have not felt sorrow without reason.
- I have not assaulted anyone.
- I am not deceitful.
- I have not stolen anyone's land.
- I have not been an eavesdropper.
- I have not falsely accused anyone.
- I have not been angry without reason.
- I have not seduced anyone's wife

THESE TEACHINGS PROVIDE A GREAT SPIRITUAL FOUNDATION

- I have not polluted myself.
- I have not terrorized anyone.
- I have not disobeyed the Law.
- I have not been exclusively angry.
- I have not cursed God/Goddess.
- I have not behaved with violence.
- I have not caused disruption of peace.
- I have not acted hastily or without thought.
- I have not overstepped my boundaries of concern.

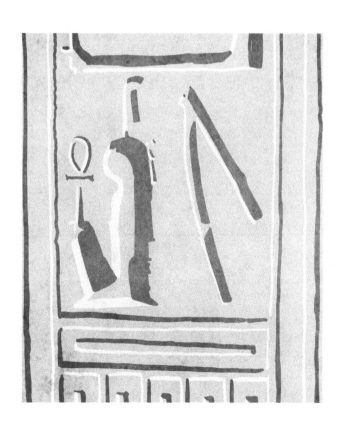

THESE TEACHINGS PROVIDE A GREAT SPIRITUAL FOUNDATION

- I have not exaggerated my words when speaking.
- I have not worked evil.
- I have not used evil thoughts, words or deeds.
- I have not polluted the water.
- I have not spoken angrily or arrogantly.
- I have not cursed anyone in thought, word or deeds.
- I have not placed myself on a pedestal.
- I have not stolen what belongs to God/Goddess.
- I have not stolen from or disrespected the deceased.
- I have not taken food from a child.
- I have not acted with insolence.
- I have not destroyed property belonging to God/Goddess.

How did we lose these teachings?

- The change from leadership and worship of Amun to monotheism by Ahkenaten weakened the Kemetic Empire to then be conquered.
- Racial slavery and white supremacy were inserted into Judaism, Christianity, and Islam.
- Slavery did not exist in MAAT.
- Through Colonialism.
- Through Miseducation.

WHY DO BLACK MEN BATTLE THE NEGATIVE STEREOTYPES

- Feelings of Weakness?
- Feeling of Irresponsible?
- Other negative Feelings?

Slavery and the Willie Lynch Letter

- This infamous letter outlines the thinking that took place during slavery in America and globally.
- It outlines how slaves were to be "broken, seasoned and conditioned."

Willie Lynch

• Slave owners must develop a way to "break" slaves.
• There were three components to this plan:
-Fear
-Distrust
-Envy

Lynch Strategy no 1: Create Division

- Light Skin vs. Dark Skin.
- White Servants (working class) vs All Black Slaves.
- Old vs. Young.
- Male vs. Females.
- Field Negro vs. House Negro.
- In the end, all of them should love, respect and trust only the white master.

LYNCH STRATEGY NO 2: "BREAKING"

- To break a horse, one must reduce it from its natural state in nature.
- Must create a situation where they are dependent instead of independent.
- Must refer to them by a non-human name – the "n" word.
- Must take their mind but keep their body.

"Breaking/Seasoning"

•Focus on the female and children first.
•A mother will naturally protect her children.
•A mother will train her children to behave in a
 way that will ensure longevity.

"Breaking/Seasoning"

- Take the most restless slave and gather the others around to watch.
- Strip him.
- Tar and Feather him.
- Set him on fire.
- Beat him.
- Do not kill him.
- This will cause fear in the hearts of those that watch.

"Breaking/Seasoning"

- A mother will not want her children to be the next one tortured this way.
- Must constantly test the females to make sure that they will submit to owners' every demand.
- Must teach female slaves to distrust male slaves--she must raise her children alone.

"Breaking/Seasoning"

- The female slave will raise her sons to be physically strong but mentally weak and dependent (for safety reasons).
- Her daughters will be raised to do the same thing she is doing.
- Female slaves who do not submit must be beaten almost to death (do not kill them as they are an investment).
- Make sure to keep male slaves away from their offspring and the female mate.

"BREAKING"

- Never allow the slaves to truly marry or form a family unit.
- Feel free to mate with female slaves so as to add "good white blood" to their offspring.

"BREAKING"

- Create a new language -- it is important that Black slaves remain foreigners in this land.
- Teach them to "talk Black" so that if they ever escape they will not make it in the world.
- Society values those who are well spoken.

Lynch Strategy no 3: Reward System

- Have the master/overseer give the slave everything that he/she needs to survive.
- Create a slave hierarchy based upon compliance to slave culture.
- Dish out rewards/punishment to those who comply vs those who fail to meet expectations.

Reward System

- Have slaves willing to go against human nature in order to receive rewards.
- All decisions made are done by the master/overseer.
- Master/overseer's authority is higher than a slave's parents.
- Break up families as needed.

What was "Ten Little N°ggers?"

- A racist nursery rhyme used historically in England to teach children how to count.

TEN little n*gger boys going out to dine;
One chocked his little self, and then
there were nine.

NINE little n*gger boys staying up too late;
One overslept himself, and then there were
eight.

EIGHT little n*gger boys going to Devon;
One said he'd stay there, and then there
were seven.

SEVEN little n*gger boys chopping up sticks;
One chopped himself in half, and then there
were six.

SIX little n*gger boys playing round a hive;
A bumble-bee stung one, and then there were
five.

FIVE little n*gger boys going in for Law;
One Got in Chancery, and Then There Were
Four.

FOUR little n*gger boys going out to sea;
A red herring swallowed one, and then there
were three.

THREE little n*gger boys walking in the zoo;
A big bear hugged one, and then there were
two.

TWO little n*gger boys sitting in the sun;
One got frizzled up, and then there was one.

One little n*gger boy living all alone;
He got married, and then they were none.

This is why we should never use this word Nigger since it was used against Black people in a negative way for so many generations.

How do we break the history that still affects us today, to become a successful Black Man?

"We must Emancipate ourselves from Mental Slavery"

"We are going to emancipate ourselves from mental slavery, for though others may free the body, none but ourselves can free the mind. Mind is our only ruler; sovereign."

-Marcus Garvey-

FOLLOW THE ORIGINAL TEACHINGS OF MAAT AND THE 10 COMMANDMENTS

What are the 10 Commandments?

- You shall have no other gods before Me.
- You shall not make for yourself a carved image—any likeness of anything that is in heaven above, or that is in the earth beneath, or that is in the water under the earth; you shall not bow down to them nor serve them.
- You shall not take the name of the LORD your God in vain.
- Remember the Sabbath day, to keep it holy. Six days you shall labor and do all your work, but the seventh day is the Sabbath of the LORD your God. Therefore the LORD blessed the Sabbath day and hallowed it.
- Honor your father and your mother, that your days may be long upon the land which the LORD your God is giving you.
- You shall not murder.
- You shall not commit adultery.
- You shall not steal.
- You shall not bear false witness against your neighbor.
- You shall not covet your neighbor's house; you shall not covet your neighbor's wife.

Beware of the First Commandment

- "I am the Lord thy God, thou shalt not have any strange gods before Me."
- This commandment excludes polytheism, the belief in many gods, insisting instead on monotheism, the belief in one God.
- This commandment disconnects Black men and women from the image and worship of the God Ausar and Goddess Auset from the great African civilizations and the female deity of MAAT whose laws governed and lifted up and respected women.

Who are some of the Gods that we learned from back in Ancient Kemet and Kush?

Ausar

Ausar was one of Egypt's most important deities. He also symbolized death, resurrection, and the cycle of Nile floods that Kemet relied on for agricultural fertility.

According to the myth, Osirus (Greek name for Ausar) was a king of Egypt who was murdered and dismembered by his brother Seth. His wife, Isis (Greek name for Auset), reassembled his body and resurrected him, allowing them to conceive a son, the god Horus (Greek name for Heru).

AUSET

Auset nursing Horus, next to Ausar

As the devoted wife who resurrected Osiris after his murder and raised their son, Horus, Isis embodied the traditional Egyptian virtues of a wife and mother.
As the wife of the god, it is believed the depictions with the infant Horus influenced Christian imagery of Mary with the infant Jesus.

HERU

Depicted as a falcon or as a man with a falcon's head, Heru was a sky god associated with war and hunting. He was also the embodiment of the divine kingship, and in some eras the reigning king was considered to be a manifestation of Heru.

According to the Ausar story, Heru was the son of Auset and Ausar, magically conceived after the murder of Ausar by his brother Seth. Heru was raised to avenge his father's murder.

PTAH

Ptah was the head of a triad of gods worshipped at Memphis. The other two members of the triad were Ptah's wife, the lion-headed goddess Sekhmet, and the god Nefertem, who may have been the couple's son.

Ptah's original association seems to have been with craftsmen and builders. The 4th-dynasty architect Imhotep was deified after his death as a son of Ptah.

Ra

The sun god Re (Ra),
one of the creator gods of ancient Egypt

One of several deities associated with the sun, the god Ra was usually represented with a human body and the head of a hawk. It was believed that he sailed across the sky in a boat each day and then made a passage through the underworld each night, during which he would have to defeat the snake god Apopis in order to rise again.

HATHOR

The goddess Hathor was usually depicted as a woman with cow's ears. Hathor embodied motherhood and fertility, and it was believed that she protected women in childbirth. She also had an important funerary aspect, being known as "the lady of the west." (Tombs were generally built on the west bank of the Nile.) In some traditions, she would welcome the setting sun every night; living people hoped to be welcomed into the afterlife in the same way.

ANUBIS

Anubis weighing the soul of the scribe Ani

Anubis was concerned with funerary practices and the care of the dead. He was usually represented as a jackal or as a man with the head of a jackal. The association of jackals with death and funerals likely arose because Egyptians would have observed jackals scavenging around cemeteries.

THOTH

Thoth, the god of writing and wisdom, could be depicted in the form of a baboon or a sacred ibis or as a man with the head of an ibis. He was believed to have invented language and the hieroglyphic script and to serve as a scribe and adviser for the gods. As the god of wisdom, Thoth was said to possess knowledge of magic and secrets unavailable to the other gods.

Amun

Amun was worshipped locally in the southern city of Thebes. Amon was a god of the air, and the name probably means the "Hidden One." He was usually represented as a man wearing a crown with two vertical plumes.

After the rulers of Thebes rebelled against a dynasty of foreign rulers known as the Hyksos and re-established native Egyptian rule throughout Egypt, Amon received credit for their victory. In a form merged with the sun god Re, he became the most powerful deity in Egypt, a position he retained for most of the New Kingdom.

Today the massive temple complex devoted to Amon-Re at Karnak is one of the most visited monuments in Egypt.

WHY IS IT IMPORTANT TO FOLLOW MAAT AND THE 10 COMMANDMENTS?

•If everyone followed these teachings the prisons would be empty and people would live with peace of mind.

Why is it important to seek Education Knowledge and Skills?

- A Black man prides himself on seeking knowledge and education, even if he doesn't have much to begin with.
- Don't love being ignorant and think it's OK to be illiterate and only how to dribble a basketball alone. Also learn the process to own a basketball franchise.
- The Black man wants to be taken seriously most of the time, don't feel the need to be paid to be a clown.
- Follow your passion and be the best you can be and try to improve upon your craft and skill everyday. Keep up with advances and innovation and try to make unique contributions.

TEACH THEM WHILE THEY ARE YOUNG IT STARTS AT HOME WITH WHO THEY ARE & RAISE THEM WITH THE KNOWLEDGE OF SELF.
-MALCOLM X-

Why is it important to Build Wealth? Own your own business? Invest?

- A Black man saves and invests money to build wealth for his family, he might even start his own business. He does not brag to you about how he spent $1,000 at the club last night and be seen throwing money in the air. Don't live paycheck-to-paycheck.

- A Black man seeks to be financially strong and independent so he can be a good provider. Don't spends your money as soon as you obtain it. Don't leave nothing but debt for your children. Leave your kids a legacy.

- Create a savings account, invest in appreciating as sets like a home and real estate.

- Invest in index ETF stock index funds/Bond funds regularly with dollar cost averaging to create wealth for your retirement.

Support Black Businesses in Your Community

- A Black man supports Black – owned companies so they can create jobs for other Black people.
- Don't think Black businesses are second-rate and spend all your money on expensive material items that depreciate with time.
- 2 billion dollars was spent on Air Jordan's recently.
- Invest yourself with education and in appreciating assets such as a home and appropriately valued real estate.

THIS IS WHY BLACKS HAVE NO POWER!!

THIS IS NOT BLACKS POWER!!

THIS IS!

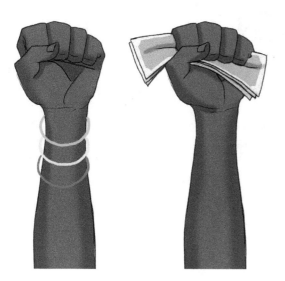

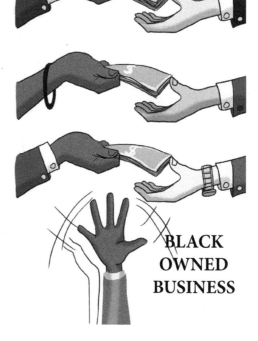

BLACK OWNED BUSINESS

THINGS YOU MUST TRY TO DO!

- Graduate High School/College/Professional School, this leads to less unemployment and greater wealth.
- People with degrees are more likely to have money to live the lives they enjoy.

THINGS YOU MUST TRY TO DO!

- Get married after you know your potential spouse for 3 years.
- This will ensure your truly know each other and will provide a solid foundation for a life together.
- Do not have children until you are married.
- Try not to get divorced.
- Getting divorced can allow you lose ½ of you wealth and lose access to your children.

Both Marriage and Education Are Highly Effecive In Reducing Child Poverty In The United States.

SUPPORT YOUR FAMILY AND KIDS

- A Black man takes care of his children, providing them with the love, guidance and support they need.
- Don't abandon your kids.
- Plan for your kids future and education.
- Have a life insurance policy for your kids.
- Start a 529K educational savings account.
- Start a Roth 401K.

DON'T DO DRUGS!

Consequences of substance abuse include:
- Addiction, unhealthy lifestyles and behaviors.
- Impaired professional and social functioning.
- Legal problems.
- Financial loss.
- Potential for criminal activity and incarceration.

Avoid Incarceration

- A Black man lives a productive lifestyle and avoids incarceration.
- Incarceration leads to more difficulty with employment. If he is incarcerated, he uses this experience to gain a chance for redemption and an opportunity to help other young men learn from his mistakes.
- Going to jail is not a badge of honor.
- Learn from your mistakes.
- Don't make your parents go broke bailing you out of jail for thousands of dollars doing something you should not have done.

Avoid Incarceration

- Blacks receive sentences 10% longer than whites.
- 13% of African American Men cannot vote because they have a felony conviction.
- After prison wage growth occurs 21% lower for Blacks compared to whites.

AVOID INCARCERATION

FIGURE 10.

Effect Of Juvenile Incarceration On Likelihood Of High School Graduation And Adult Imprisonment

Juvenile incarceration reduces the likelihood of high school graduationby more than 13 percentage points, and increases the probability of returnig to prison as an adult by over 22 percentage points, as compared to nondetaimed juvenile offenders.

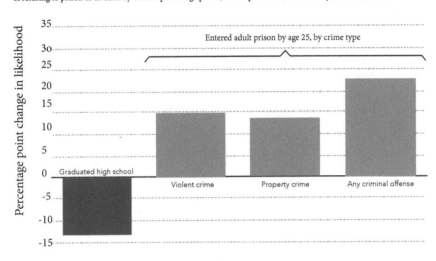

Source: Aizer and Doyle 2013,
Note: Bars show statistically significant regression estimates of the causual effect of juvenile incarceration of high school completion and on adult recidivisme. For more details, see the technical appendix.

Avoid Incarceration

- A criminal record can reduce the likelihood of a callback or job offer by nearly 50 percent. The negative impact of a criminal record is twice as large for African American applicants.
- Infectious diseases are highly concentrated in corrections facilities: 15% of jail inmates and 22% of prisoners – compared to 5% of the general population – reported ever having tuberculosis, Hepatitis B and C, HIV, v AIDS, or other STDS.

Respect Women and Your Mother

- A Black man is disciplined about his sexual choices.
- It is natural to like women.
- A real man respects women.
- Don't have a flock of women.
- Know your HIV status.

-Malcolm X for quote-

"THE BLACK MAN WILL NEVER GET ANYBODY'S RESPECT UNTIL HE FIRST LEARNS TO RESPECT HIS OWN WOMEN"

Boom. But most of all need to create that environment to be respected.

LEARN FROM YOUR MISTAKES

- A Black man, despite his mistakes, seeks to grow as a person and become more responsible.
- Don't live in your mother's basement and assume somebody else is going to take care of your kids.
- Don't play video games on the living room couch until you're 40 years old.

Legally protect your community

- A Black man is willing to take up arms to defend his community and protect his children.
- Don't take up arms to go kill another Black man.
- Don't fight over something stupid, like a man stepping on his shoes at the club or giving him a funny look.

TAKE A STAND AGAINST RACISM.

- A Black man is, quite simply, a MAN:
- Take a stand against racism, protect your family and community.
- Don't be silent and think that the Black man I've just described is "acting white."

We live in a capitalistic world!

- Being the business owner, land owner and home owner makes you more successful.
- Being a laborer and renter may not make you as successful unless you have a desirable skills set.

Nursery Rhyme Part Two for Survival by a Mentor of Mine

Dr. Gerald Deas

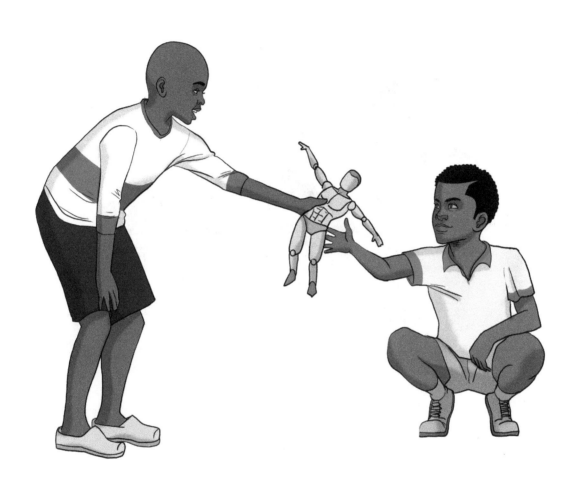

•One Little Black Boy was loved and he grew; he shared with another and then there were TWO.

•Two little Black boys learned to agree; with the help of one another, then there were THREE.

•Three Black Teenage Boys learned to do even more; they lifted one who had fallen and then there were FOUR.

•Four young Black Men learned how to survive; they joined hands with another and then there were FIVE.

•Five young Black Men built with mortar and bricks; they encouraged another builder, and then there were SIX.

•Six Black Brothers knew Hell from Heaven; they turned another brother around and then there were SEVEN.

•Seven Black Students learned never to be late;
a serious brother followed them and there were
EIGHT.

•Eight Black Men became strong with time;
they linked arms with another, and then there
were NINE.

•Nine Little Black Boys became strong men; they looked for a leader, and then there were TEN.

•Ten Little Black Boys are only a few:

TO BECOME STRONG MEN AND WOMEN
WILL BE UP TO YOU!

THANK YOU FOR YOUR TIME AND SUPPORT!

This is the first edition if you have thoughts or comments to improve this book I would love to hear from you and can email me at dlarochemd@aol.com

If you liked the book and you would like to sponsor copies for other young men please send your contributions via PayPal to dlarochemd@aol.com. Thank you.

SUGGESTED FURTHER READING

- *Blacks in Science: Ancient and Modern,* by Ivan Van Sertima

- *Christopher Columbus and the Afrikan Holocaust: Slavery and the Rise of European Capitalism,* by Dr. John Henrik Clarke

- *The Teachings of Ptahhotep: The Oldest Book in the World,* by Dr. Asa G Hilliard III, Larry Williams

- *Marcus Garvey and the Vision of Africa,* by Dr. John Henrik Clarke

- *They Came Before Columbus: The African Presence in Ancient America* (Journal of African Civilizations) by Dr. Ivan Van Sertima

- *7 Little White Lies: The Conspiracy to Destroy the Black Self-Image,* by Mr. Jabari G Osaze

- *The Isis Papers: The Keys to the Colors,* by Dr. Frances Cress Welsing

- *Chronicle of the Pharaohs: The Reign-By-Reign Record of the Rulers and Dynasties of Ancient Egypt* With 350 Illustrations 130 in Color, by Peter A. Clayton

- *Philosophy And Opinions Of Marcus Garvey,* by Marcus Garvey

- *The Autobiography of Malcolm X,* by Alex Haley and Malcolm X

DISCUSSION QUESTIONS

1. After reading this book, how do you feel you will navigate through life differently?

2. If you occasionally use the N-word, how do you feel about using it now after reading this book?

3. Has your sense of self-worth changed after reading this book? If so, how?

4. How do the Divine Principles of MAAT compare to the 10 Commandments? What are your thoughts about their similarities?

5. What can you do today to change the negative stereotypes of black men?

6. What have been some of the residual impacts of slavery on black men today?

7. How are you going to pay forward the lessons learned in this book in your community?

8. Do you have an idea for a business that could build wealth in the black community? If yes, please share. What resources do you think you will need to get your business started?

9. What do you believe the role of education will play in changing the trajectory of black men?

10. Now that marijuana is being legalized, how do you believe the non-medical use will impact the black community? Do you see this as an opportunity or just another way for another group of people to take advantage of the black community?

11. Do you have a friend that you would want to share the book with? If so why?

CPSIA information can be obtained
at www.ICGtesting.com
Printed in the USA
BVHW011149081022
648962BV00004B/4